K is for Kick

A Soccer Alphabet

Written by Brad Herzog and Illustrated by Melanie Rose

Sleeping Bear Press™

2395 South Huron Parkway, Suite 200
Ann Arbor, MI 48104
www.sleepingbearpress.com

Printed and bound in China.

10 9 8 7 6 5 4 3 2 1 (case)
10 9 8 7 6 (pbk)

Library of Congress Cataloging-in-Publication Data
Herzog, Brad.
K is for kick : a soccer alphabet / by Brad Herzog ;
illustrated by Melanie Rose.
p. cm.
Summary: Examines the history and lore of soccer from A for a game
played "all over the world" to Z for "Zinedine Zidane," a French star
named the world's best.

ISBN 978-1-58536-130-4 (case)   ISBN 978-1-58536-339-1 (pbk)

1. Soccer-Juvenile literature. 2. Alphabet books. [1. Soccer.
2. Alphabet.] I. Rose, Melanie, ill. II. Title.
GV943.25 .H47 2003
796.334—dc21   2003010465

Millions of people of all ages and on every continent play soccer. More than a billion people watch the men's World Cup finals on television. The group that helps set and revise the rules of the game is the Federation Internationale de Football Association or FIFA (pronounced "FEE-fuh"). It was established in 1904. Soccer is such a global passion that people will play anywhere. In 1995, two teams from Russia played a game at the North Pole, where the temperature was 20 degrees below zero.

A is where soccer is played
all over the world,
in almost any country
with a flag proudly unfurled.

From Argentina to Australia,
you'll find a soccer goal.
Even on the Arctic ice,
way up at the North Pole.

A a

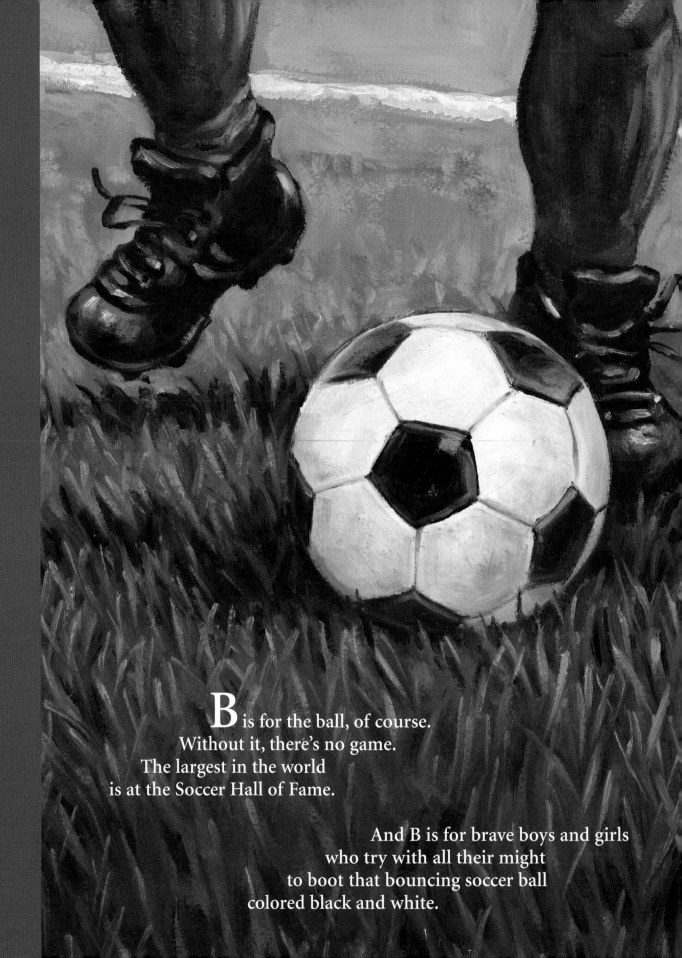

Aside from the massive sculpted ball that appears to be crashing through an exterior wall of the National Soccer Hall of Fame in Oneonta, New York, the facility also includes historical displays and a kids' indoor field. The Hall of Fame has one of the world's largest collections of soccer artifacts, featuring more than 80,000 items. But the heart of the Hall is the room honoring the more than 220 inductees—players, coaches, trainers, officials, and administrators. The Canadian Soccer Hall of Fame and Museum is in Vaughn, Ontario.

Soccer rules call for the ball to be round and made of leather or other approved materials. It should weigh between 14 and 16 ounces and should measure between 27 and 28 inches around.

Soccer in the U.S. officially began in 1913 when the United States Football Association (now called the U.S. Soccer Federation) was formed. The following year saw the arrival of the first national tournament—the National Challenge Cup in the U.S. The founding meeting of the Dominion of Canadian Football was held in Toronto on May 24, 1912 when provincial soccer executives laid the foundation of what is today's Canadian Soccer Association.

B is for the ball, of course.
Without it, there's no game.
The largest in the world
is at the Soccer Hall of Fame.

And B is for brave boys and girls
who try with all their might
to boot that bouncing soccer ball
colored black and white.

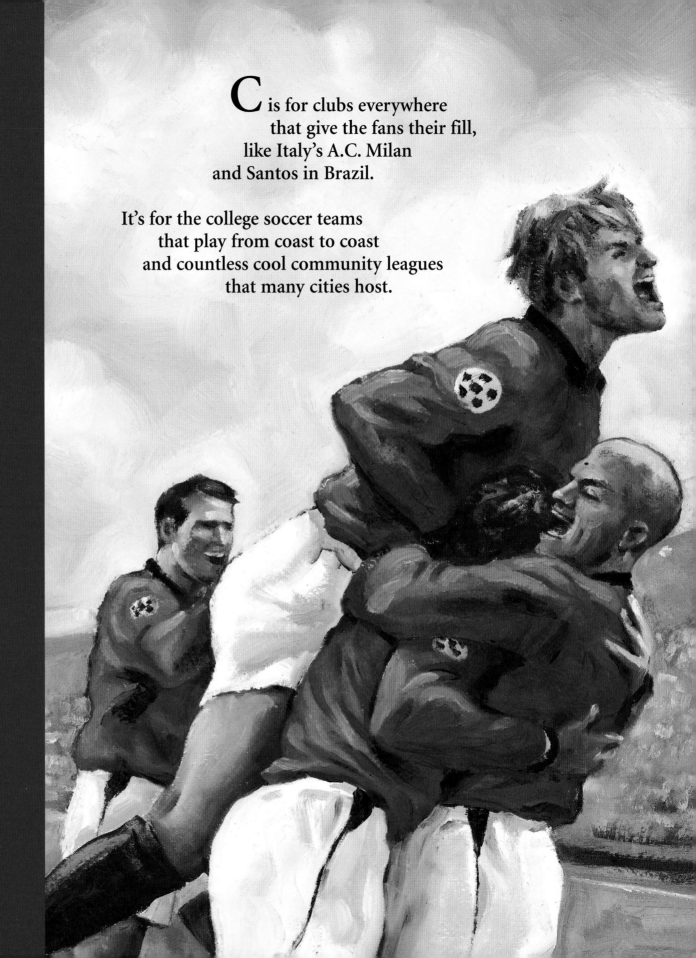

Most countries in Europe and Latin America have professional or semiprofessional soccer leagues. The winner of the top division is the country's national champion. Many of these top teams compete against other country's top teams. Among the champions over the years are legendary clubs such as England's Manchester United, Spain's Real Madrid, and Italy's A.C. Milan.

Soccer at the university level, like soccer elsewhere in North America, grew slowly until the 1960s. Today, there are Division I, II, and III college championships for both men and women.

C is for clubs everywhere
that give the fans their fill,
like Italy's A.C. Milan
and Santos in Brazil.

It's for the college soccer teams
that play from coast to coast
and countless cool community leagues
that many cities host.

Defenders, also called fullbacks, are the last line of defense in front of the goalkeeper. Their primary mission is to take the ball from the other team, but defenders also begin their own team's offense. Defenders try to get the ball and pass it to a teammate. The stopper is the defensive player responsible for making sure the other team's top-scoring player doesn't succeed. The sweeper roams from side to side, sweeping the area clear of the ball that has gotten by other defenders.

D is also dribbling (moving the ball by controlling it with your feet) and "Diego's Wonder." In 1986, Diego Maradona led Argentina's national team to the World Cup title. After dribbling past, through, and around nearly the entire English team during a World Cup game, Maradona left the goaltender sprawled on the grass as he kicked the ball into an open net. The goal, called "Diego's Wonder," was one of the most electrifying feats in soccer history.

D is for the defense,
deflecting shots on goal.
Each daring defender
has a special role.

Fullbacks, stoppers, sweepers...
they keep a game low scoring.
The ways they break up plays
are anything but boring.

E e

Eleven players to a side.
That's the letter **E**—
forwards, midfielders, defenders,
and the brave goalie.

E is also England,
where soccer first was played
and where excitement for the game
will likely never fade.

Midfielders, also called halfbacks, dribble and pass the ball looking for scoring chances. Forwards are usually responsible for scoring goals. The forward, also called a striker, is the one who plays closest to the opposing team's goal. Commonly, teams use three or four forwards, two or three midfielders, and four defenders. It depends on the coach's style.

Although a game similar to soccer was played in the Far East more than 2,000 years ago, modern soccer has its roots in England. Many English schools played various versions of a kicking game in the early 1800s, but it wasn't until 1848 that a group gathered and wrote the first soccer rules. As British sailors traveled the world, they often organized soccer games, which spread the game to all parts of the globe, particularly throughout Europe and South America.

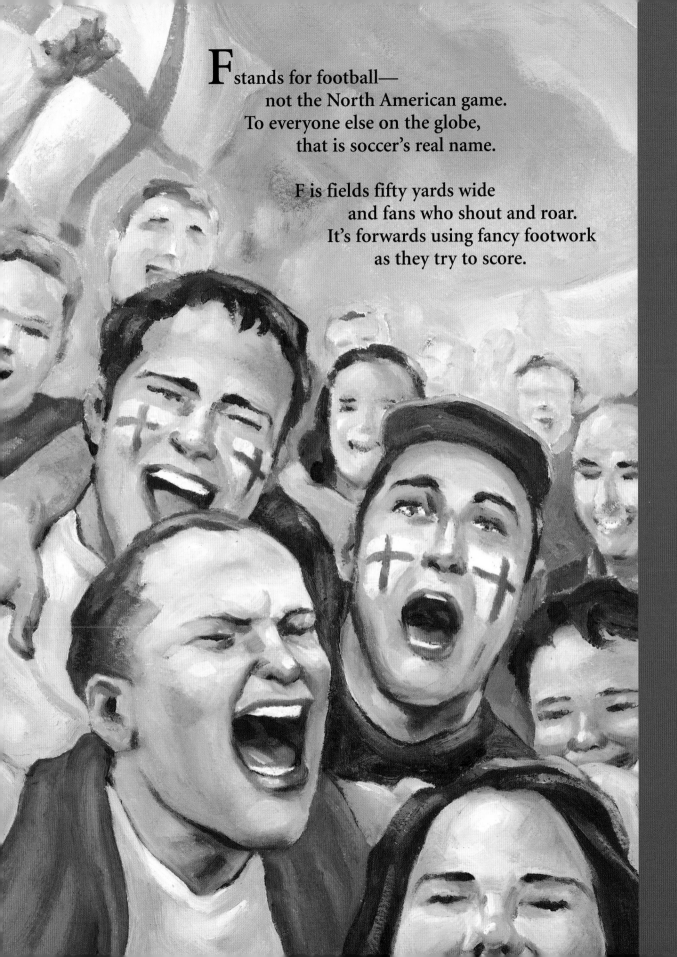

F stands for football—
    not the North American game.
To everyone else on the globe,
    that is soccer's real name.

F is fields fifty yards wide
    and fans who shout and roar.
It's forwards using fancy footwork
    as they try to score.

Soccer was originally known as "association football." In the 1860s English schoolboys liked to nickname things by adding "er" to the word. For example, rugby was often called "rugger." So "association football" was shortened to "assoc," which soon became "assoccer." Eventually this evolved into "soccer." Still, the game is called football in nearly every country except the United States and Canada.

There is no standard size for a soccer field (the British called it a soccer pitch). Rules call for the game to be played on a rectangular field that is between 100 and 130 yards long and between 50 and 100 yards wide. The boundary lines at either end of the field are goal lines, while the side boundaries are touchlines. A center circle in the middle of the field, measuring 10 yards across, with the centerline dividing it in half, is where the game begins.

Ff

G is for the goalkeeper
with one glove on each hand,
who guards the net so expertly
and makes the team's last stand.

The goal he guards is eight feet high
and 24 feet wide.
His job is to make sure
he doesn't let the ball inside.

G g

The goalkeeper is the only player on a team who may use his hands other than when a player is awarded a throw-in. He guards the goal within a rectangular penalty area that measures 44 yards wide and extends 18 yards from the goal line. The goal area is a smaller rectangle—20 yards wide and extending six yards in front of the goal. After the goalkeeper catches the ball or picks it up off the ground, it may be thrown or drop-kicked into play.

G is also for Gordon Banks and the "greatest save ever." Banks was a goalkeeper who led England to the 1966 World Cup championship. Four years later in the same tournament, his team faced Brazil and the great Pelé. Ten minutes into the game, with Banks standing near the left post of his goal, Pelé headed a ball toward the right side of the net. Banks dived the full width of the goal and managed to get a hand on the ball. It flew over the goal—history's greatest save.

H is for using your head
to redirect a shot.
Hand balls are illegal,
but hard heads are not.

Just watch the ball soar your way,
time your leap just right
and hope your noggin meets
the soccer ball in flight.

A "header" is to strike the ball using one's head. A header may be a defensive play, such as clearing the ball, or it may be offensive, such as a pass or a shot on goal. Two of soccer's best at heading were Hungary's Sandor Kocsis, who was the top scorer at the 1954 World Cup, and West Germany's Uwe Seeler, who scored using the header shot in four different World Cup tournaments. Both were nicknamed "The Golden Head."

It has been estimated that a soccer player heads the ball an average of six times per game and many more times during practice. So proper technique, such as trying to use the thickest part of the skull (the forehead) to head the ball, is important to prevent head injuries.

A "hand ball" is not allowed in soccer, but the term "hand" actually includes any part of the arm below the armpit. Only the goaltender may use his hands. If another player uses hands, the other team is awarded a direct free kick from where the hand touched the ball.

H
h

The first recorded indoor soccer match took place in Canada in 1885 when two teams faced off in a roller skating rink. Today, many indoor fields around the country have been built specifically for the game.

The number of players per side varies in indoor soccer according to the league and the size of the field. Indoor games are usually divided into four 15-minute quarters, and coaches can substitute players any time during the game, as often as needed to allow tired players time to rest. Like hockey, players are sent to a penalty box for major fouls. And like basketball, there is a three-point arc. A goal scored from more than 45 feet away is worth three points.

I i

Indoor soccer—
    that's our choice for the letter I.
The pace is fast and furious.
    The scores are rather high.

            The game is often played
                on turf inside a hockey rink.
            A goal could happen any time,
            so indoor fans don't blink.

J j

J is for the jerseys
    soccer players wear.
        But often in big matches,
            opponents tend to share.

In a gesture of respect
    after a game ends,
        they simply swap their jerseys
            as if they are old friends.

In the world of soccer, an international exhibition match is often called a "friendly." Nothing supports this term more than the traditional practice of swapping jerseys with a worthy opponent at the end of a match. Often, players put on their opponent's jersey immediately, right on the field.

This postgame tradition has been credited to Brazilian superstar Pelé, who offered his jersey to England's captain Bobby Moore after the 1970 World Cup final. Moore offered his jersey in return, and a tradition began.

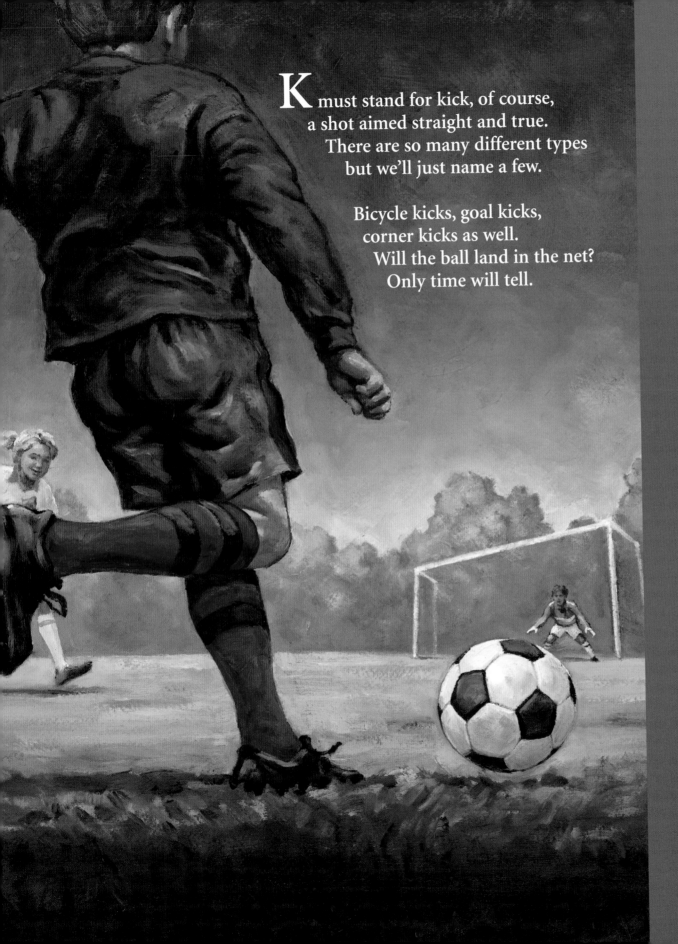

K must stand for kick, of course,
a shot aimed straight and true.
There are so many different types
but we'll just name a few.

Bicycle kicks, goal kicks,
corner kicks as well.
Will the ball land in the net?
Only time will tell.

A bicycle kick is an acrobatic shot in which a player kicks the ball in midair backward and over his own head. It is one of the most athletic and exciting moves in soccer. Longtime U.S. national team star Marcelo Balboa was famous for bicycle kicks, including one shot during the 2000 Major League Soccer season that was voted Goal of the Year.

If the attacking team kicks the ball over the goal line (but not into the goal), the defending team is awarded a goal kick. Goal kicks are taken from within the goal area and must travel beyond the penalty area and are usually taken by the goal-keeper but any player can take the kick.

If the defensive team kicks the ball over the goal line, the opposing team is awarded a corner kick from the quarter-circle mark where the goal line and touchline meet. The kicker boots the ball into the goal area. Many goals are scored in this manner, usually by teammates timing the pass and heading the ball into the goal.

k

K

L is for the ladies
who play the game they love.
The U.S. women's national team
is a cut above.

In 1999,
a jam-packed Rose Bowl crowd,
watched them win the World Cup
and cheered them long and loud.

An official U.S. women's soccer team wasn't established until 1985, but quickly American women have proved themselves the best in the world with victories in the first-ever Women's World Cup (in 1991) and the first one held in the U.S. (in 1999), as well as a gold medal at the 1996 Summer Olympics, celebrated with 92,000 screaming fans.

In 1980, just over 40,000 girls played high school soccer, and there were only a few dozen women's college teams. But by 2000, nearly 270,000 girls were competing in high school and nearly 800 colleges in the NCAA fielded varsity women's squads. More than 260,000 girls compete on American Youth Soccer Organization teams. During 2002 more than 307,000 girls under 18 were playing soccer in Canada. Following the excitement of the 1999 Women's World Cup, a women's professional league emerged— the Women's United Soccer Association (WUSA).

In 2000, U.S. national team legend Michelle Akers was named FIFA's Women's Player of the Century.

When the United States was awarded the honor of hosting the 1994 World Cup, it was on the condition that a professional league would be established in America. In 1996 Major League Soccer (MLS) began in the U.S. In Canada, the National Soccer League (Later the Canadian National Soccer League) was the top league in Canada. The Canadian Professional Soccer League that started in 1997 replaced it.

M is also the Magnificent Magyars, the nickname of the Hungarian national team led by captain Ferenc Puskas, who was known as the "Galloping Major." Hungary went undefeated in 34 straight international matches from 1950 to 1954 before losing to West Germany in the 1954 World Cup Finals.

M is Major League Soccer
and all the soccer pros
who make their mark on U.S. soil
against talented foes.

The Mutiny, the Galaxy,
the Burn, the Clash, the Crew.
The MetroStars, the Fusion,
the Revolution, too.

m
M

The University of North Carolina women's soccer team represents one of the great dynasties in the history of intercollegiate sports. Coach Anson Dorrance started the varsity program in 1979. Two years later, the Tar Heels won their first national title. They went on to win 17 more over the next 19 years. More than 60 different North Carolina players have earned All-America honors, and nearly 40 of them have gone on to play for the U.S. national team.

N is also for number 19 from North Carolina—Mia Hamm, the finest and most recognized women's soccer player in the world. Hamm's #19 jersey has been retired, meaning no other female soccer player can wear #19 at the University of North Carolina. She has played on two winning World Cup teams and an Olympic gold medal team. In 1999 Hamm broke the all-time international scoring record, for men and women, with her 108th career goal.

The North Carolina women's team—
that's the letter N.
With 18 national titles
they're the best that's ever been.

Their nervous fans cheer throughout
90 minutes of fun,
never letting up
until the soccer game is won.

Only three nations competed in the first Olympic soccer event at the 1900 Summer Games in Paris. For nearly a century, only men played Olympic soccer, but the United States won the first women's Olympic competition in 1996.

Soccer games played according to international rules are divided into two 45-minute halves. If the teams are tied after 90 minutes, some leagues play one or sometimes two overtime periods to determine a winner. If the teams remain tied after the overtimes, the game is decided by a shootout—each team trading shots on goal in a series of penalty kicks.

The offside rule is meant to keep an offensive player from waiting by the goal. Generally, there must be at least two defenders (including the goalkeeper) between a player and his opponent's goal. If a player is even with a defender, then he is not offside. And if a player is onside when a pass is attempted, he can receive the pass with only the goalkeeper between him and the goal.

O is for Olympic Games,
held once every four years,
when athletes play for soccer gold
and heed their countries' cheers.

O is also overtime,
extra play when tied.
It's players running down the field
and being called offside.

Pp

P is a near-perfect player
who outperformed the rest.
Of all soccer's professionals,
Pelé was the best.

He scored more than 1,000 goals
in the U.S. and Brazil.
No person has played better.
Perhaps nobody will.

Edson Arantes do Nascimento, known throughout the world as Pelé, is widely considered the greatest male player in soccer history. He joined Brazil's national team and played in the 1958 World Cup at the age of 17. In all, during his career, Pelé recorded 97 goals in 111 international games, leading his country to three World Cup titles.

Pelé retired in 1974, but the following year he surprised the world by signing a contract with the New York Cosmos of the North American Soccer League. His arrival made soccer even more popular in the United States. His final game in 1977 was watched by more than 77,000 fans and 650 journalists and was broadcast to 38 nations on television.

P is also pass, which is when a player kicks the ball to his teammate. A pass may be used to keep the ball away from an opponent, to move the ball closer to the opposing goal or to give the ball to a player who is in a better position to score. The pass wasn't really a part of soccer until an 1872 game between England and Scotland, when the Scottish players realized they could move the ball better if they passed it back and forth.

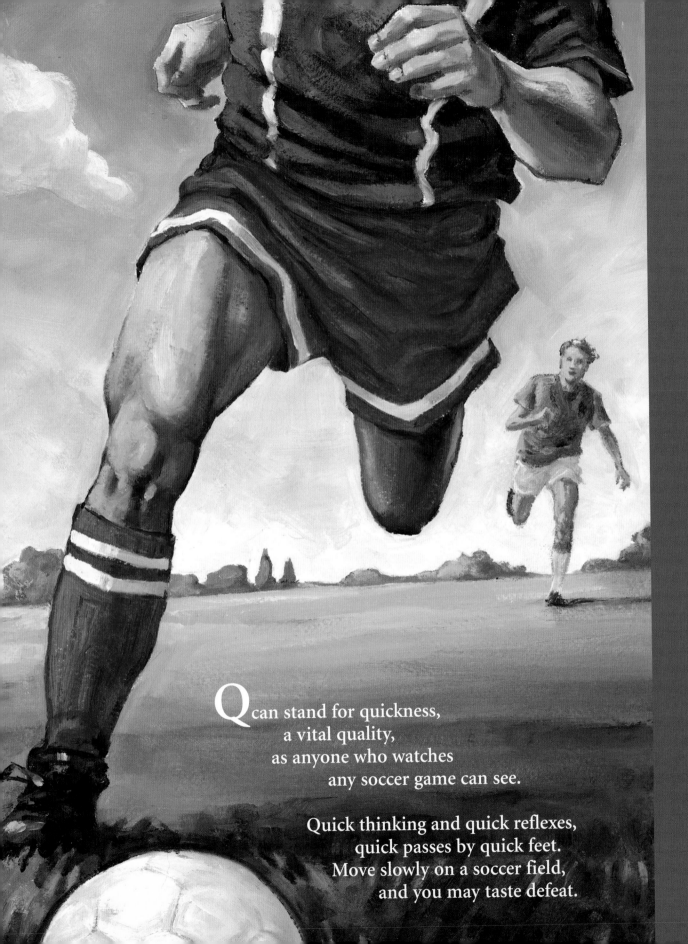

Speed is a very important part of soccer. World-class players can boot the ball at speeds of more than 70 miles per hour and dribble the ball faster than many people can run. But quick thinking and speedy reactions are also necessary during the game. For instance, a defender who is attempting to intercept a pass must consider dozens of factors in a fraction of a second. Where is the ball going? How fast is an opposing player moving toward it? What are his skills? What is the pace of the pass? Is it on the ground or in the air? Where can it be intercepted? What part of the body should be used to do so? What should be done with the ball? Head it? Trap it? Clear it? Shoot it? Pass it? To whom? To where?

Q can stand for quickness,
a vital quality,
as anyone who watches
any soccer game can see.

Quick thinking and quick reflexes,
quick passes by quick feet.
Move slowly on a soccer field,
and you may taste defeat.

R is for the referee
showing a red card.
The player who commits the foul
has to leave the yard.

The ref may flash a yellow card
when a foul stops action.
Two yellows equals one red,
a serious infraction.

R r

Most soccer games are officiated by one referee and two linesmen. Linesmen are responsible for determining which team gets possession of the ball after it goes out-of-bounds and which players are offside. The linesmen can also signal the referee when they witness a foul, but only the referee can make that call. The referee starts the game, serves as the official timekeeper, and enforces the rules.

The referee is responsible for issuing yellow and red cards. A yellow card, or caution, is a warning to a player who has committed a serious penalty, such as tripping, unsportsmanlike conduct, or entering or leaving the game without the referee's permission. A red card, or sending off, is occasionally issued to a player who exhibits serious foul play. Two yellow cards result in an automatic red card. The player must leave the game immediately.

Soccer is "the simplest game."
That's the letter S.
Don't own a ball? Use rolled-up socks.
No sport does more with less.

On city streets or sandlots,
there are many ways to play.
Many soccer superstars
started just that way.

In 1862, when a man named J.C. Thring wrote 10 rules for a sport that would become known in the United States as soccer, he called it "The Simplest Game." The object of soccer is, indeed, simple: Put the ball in your opponent's goal more often than they put it in yours.

The basic rules of soccer are so simple that the game can be played in some form almost anywhere. Parks and streets serve as makeshift soccer fields. A pair of trees or rocks or hats can be turned into goals. Imagination is an important soccer skill. In fact, one young boy in Brazil grew up in the 1940s using a grapefruit as a soccer ball. Do you know his name? Pelé.

Ss

T t

T is for trapping the ball.
No hands allowed—that's why
players stop it with their chest
or with their foot or thigh.

T can be a throw-in, too
to put the ball in play,
or a tough and tactful tackle
to take the ball away.

In soccer, a trap is how a player stops a moving ball and gains control of it without illegally using his arms or hands. A tackle is a means of getting the ball from the opponent. It may be accomplished by sliding or by a shoulder charge, and often both players fall to the ground. However, the rules do not allow elbowing, holding, pushing, tripping, or hip-checking.

When a player last touches a ball that passes over the touchline, his opponent may throw it back in play from the point where it crossed the line. The ball is thrown with both hands from behind and over the head. It is the only time a player other than the goalie is allowed to use his hands. After the throw-in, the player cannot touch the ball until it has been touched by a teammate or opponent. If the ball is improperly thrown in, a throw-in is awarded to someone from the opposite team.

In the early days of soccer, uniforms were very much different from today's lightweight jerseys and shorts. Players commonly wore knickerbockers fastened tightly below the knee, long stockings, and heavy boots. Often, players wore caps—sometimes even top hats! Eventually, these uniforms were replaced by jerseys and long shorts. Over the years, the shorts have become shorter and the clothing has become lighter.

U is for the uniforms
that most soccer teams use—
shorts and colored jerseys,
socks and cleated shoes.

And U is a brave underdog
against a mighty foe.
In soccer anything can happen.
Some days you never know.

V
V

V is for Virginia,
once Bruce Arena's team.
They challenged for the college crown
every year, it seemed.

In 2002,
the coach led the U.S.A.
to the World Cup quarterfinals—
quite a fine display.

From 1979 through 1995, Coach Bruce Arena's University of Virginia team produced a record of 295 wins, 58 losses, and 32 ties and won five national titles. In 1996, Arena coached the U.S. Olympic men's soccer team and coached the D.C. United squad to victory in the first-ever MLS Cup. Arena took over as coach of the U.S. national team in 1998 and set about developing a team that could compete with any in the world. The Americans proved it at the 2002 World Cup. The Americans' seven total goals and two wins matched its best World Cup performance since the first tournament 72 years earlier

The World Cup is a soccer tournament, held every four years for both men and women, that decides the best national team on the planet. Only 13 countries competed in the first World Cup tournament in 1930, which was by invitation only. In 2002, more than 190 nations participated in the qualifying tournament for the World Cup.

Frenchman Jules Rimet first had the idea of a World Cup competition and donated a gold trophy to be presented to the champions. When Brazil took the title for a third time in 1970, its national team was allowed to keep the Jules Rimet cup. So a new trophy, designed by an Italian sculptor, was created. It is made of 18-carat gold and shows two soccer players holding up a large globe.

W is for winners. The 17 men's World Cup tournaments held between 1930 and 2002 were won by only seven different countries. Brazil won five times, followed by Italy (3), West Germany (3), Argentina (2), Uruguay (2), England (1), and France (1).

W is the World Cup
32-team ball
to see which nation has
the finest soccer squad of all.

From Canada to Cameroon,
from India to France,
every nation wants to be
the last one at the dance.

A free kick is a shot on goal awarded after a rule violation. It can be direct or indirect. An indirect free kick is awarded for such offenses as offside violations and obstructing an opposing player. It counts as a goal only if the ball touches a player on either team before crossing the goal line.

A direct free kick counts as a goal whether or not the ball touches anyone on its way to the goal. It is awarded for major, intentional offenses, such as playing the ball with the arm or hand, tripping, pushing, or holding.

A penalty kick is a direct free kick awarded when a defender commits a major foul within his team's penalty area. The kicker places the ball at a spot determined by the referee. The goalkeeper must stand on the goal line between the goalposts and cannot move his feet until the ball is kicked. The rest of the players must remain outside the penalty area. If the goalkeeper stops the ball or it rebounds into the playing field, play continues. If the ball enters the net it is a goal!

X marks the spot
    where someone commits a foul.
A penalty kick, right then and there,
        is what the rules allow.

    The other players must remain
        at least 10 yards away.
    The extra nervous goalie
            is asked to save the day.

Y is for youth soccer,
the favorite game of all.
Happy children get their kicks
and have themselves a ball.

It's more popular around the world
than any other sport
played on a field or diamond
or in a rink or court.

Y y

Hundreds of millions of children play soccer around the world. In the United States, the sport is one of the most popular pastimes for kids under age 12. The American Youth Soccer Organization began in California in 1964 with nine teams. Today there are more than 50,000 AYSO teams in 46 states. The AYSO holds regional championships, but there are also international competitions for youth soccer players. In Canada nearly 700,000 youths under 18 registered to play soccer in 2002.

Y is also goalkeeper Lev Yashin, who led the Soviet team to an Olympic gold medal in 1956 and a European Championship in 1960. As the star of the Dinamo Moscow club team, he was named European Player of the Year in 1963. A quarter-century later, a panel of 250 international soccer journalists chose Yashin as the lone goalkeeper on the World Team of the 20th Century.

Midfielder Zinedine Zidane has twice been named FIFA World Player of the Year, in 1998 and 2000. Zidane recorded two goals against Brazil in the final game to lead France to the 1998 World Cup crown. Four years later he scored a brilliant left-footed goal from the edge of the penalty area to lift his Real Madrid club team to the European Cup championship.

Z is also record-setting Italian goaltender Dino Zoff, who set what is perhaps an unbreakable international shutout mark in 1974 by playing 1,143 minutes—or more than 12 straight games—without allowing a goal. He led his club team, Juventus, to five league titles. Then, at age 41 in 1982, he captained Italy to the World Cup championship.

Z z

Z is Zinedine Zidane,
a French star named world's best,
and athletes of all ages
who play the game with zest.

A pass that zips across the field,
a game tied 0-0,
and catching Z's while dreaming
of being a soccer hero.

Brad Herzog

Brad Herzog began his writing career as a sports reporter at a small newspaper in upstate New York, where soccer was one of his beats. The 34-year-old freelance writer has since published more than a dozen books, as well as hundreds of magazine articles on topics ranging from the civil rights movement to sports car racing and from Pez to Zen.

A past Grand Gold Medal Award winner from the Council for Advancement and Support of Education, Brad has written several fiction and nonfiction children's books for various educational publishers. He is also the author of *The Sports 100*, which ranks the 100 most important people in U.S. sports history (Pelé was #90). Brad's travel narrative, *States of Mind*, was chosen as one of the 10 outstanding books from independent publishers in 1999.

Melanie Rose

Melanie lives in Mississauga, Canada with her son Liam, and their two cats, Mickey and Meesha. Melanie also illustrated *M is for Maple: A Canadian Alphabet* and *Z is for Zamboni: A Hockey Alphabet*. She is a graduate of the Ontario College of Art.